LESSONS *from the* FATHER'S CLASSROOM

A Journey of Faith

KERRI ESTES

WESTBOW
PRESS®
A DIVISION OF THOMAS NELSON
& ZONDERVAN

Unless otherwise noted, all scripture is from the
New King James Version of the Bible.

Scripture quotations marked NKJV are from the New King James Version of the
Bible © 1982 by Thomas Nelson, Inc. Used by permission. All rights reserved.

WestBow Press books may be ordered through booksellers or by contacting:

WestBow Press
A Division of Thomas Nelson & Zondervan
1663 Liberty Drive
Bloomington, IN 47403
www.westbowpress.com
1 (866) 928-1240

ISBN: 978-1-5127-0069-5 (sc)
ISBN: 978-1-5127-0068-8 (e)

Print information available on the last page.

WestBow Press rev. date: 11/09/2015

Table of Contents

PREFACE

At this moment, I am completely full. It's funny because I just finished pouring my heart out to a friend. How ironic it is that when we are poured out, we are filled simultaneously. Life works like that, because we were created for companionship, designed for each other; so fulfillment is found when we share the overflow of our own hearts with others. It is for that reason that I'm writing.

Throughout my journey with God, I've learned many lessons. I hope that by sharing my experiences and revelations with others, I can help them to realize those same lessons . . . lessons of wisdom, guidance, strength and intimacy with God. These lessons were not learned from scholarly individuals or physical institutions. They are straight from the Father's classroom.

I am writing especially for my children, so that they can have a glimpse into the journey of my life as they began to explore their own journeys. I want to leave a legacy for them through my writing and share with them the many ways that God has revealed Himself to me personally, encouraging them to develop a very strong, personal relationship with their heavenly Father.

Every time I read over these experiences that God has brought me through and these lessons He has taught me, I'm reminded of His constant companionship, His unfailing mercy and His limitless power and authority in my life. I hope that these words, these stories and lessons will encourage, inspire and empower you as you grow in your relationship with Jesus Christ.

CHAPTER 1

If God gives you a bridge, it isn't walking on water!

". . I tell you the truth, if you have faith as small as a mustard seed, you can say to this mountain, 'Move from here to there' and it will move. Nothing will be impossible for you." Matthew 17:20 NIV

P erhaps one of the greatest faith stories of the New Testament is the story of Peter walking on the water. We can learn so much from Peter's experience. He was able to do the impossible at Jesus' command, "Come." Peter stepped out of the safety and security of the boat to walk on top of a stormy sea . . . . and he was successful! Peter was doing the impossible . . . until he took his eyes off Jesus. He looked at the storm. As soon as Peter realized the absurdity of his position from the human perspective, he began to sink. He was no longer focused on Jesus. We learn from Peter that when we look at our circumstances instead of at God, we will fail. Faith ends where fear begins, because fear compels us to rely on our own strengths and abilities instead of leaning on God.

My preacher friend, Tim Staire, once preached a very powerful message on this topic during a revival in my church. He called it *Get out of the boat!* He shared that we have to get out of our comfort zone and take a step forward in faith if we want to grow. We have to leave behind those "comfortable" things that drag us down and trust that God has better things for us.

At the time of this message, I was really struggling with a past relationship. It had dwindled to nearly nothing, but I was hanging on to the strings that remained. I was in my first year of college and felt that I was losing the "love of my life." During Bro. Staire's message, I felt God beckoning me to "let it go" and "step out of the boat in faith." I knew that God had great things in store for me, but I just couldn't see how I could ever be happy without the relationship I was so desperately clinging to. While I said that I trusted God's plan for my life, I was, in fact, questioning it. I thought I knew what I needed. I knew what my heart was saying, and I was allowing those feelings to guide me rather than submitting to God's truth. The truth was and is that He has good plans for my life, not plans to harm me, but plans to give me a hopeful future. (Jeremiah 29:11 paraphrased) I would say to God, "Let Your will be done, but please don't make me let 'him' go." I wanted to be all that God was calling me to be, wanted to do great things for Him, but just could not let go of the comfortable, the familiar, what *I* thought I needed. God wanted me to trust Him with all the details of His plan for me. He wanted me to just let go and allow Him to lead me.

On that night in revival, as I heard God gently calling to me to get out of the boat, to step away from that relationship into something deeper, my response to God was, "Okay. I'll let go. Just show me that there's someone else for me, and I will let go of him for good." God sharply replied back in my spirit, "If I give you a bridge, it isn't walking on water." God calls us to step out in faith, so that we can learn to trust Him. Only then can He do the wonderful things He desires to do in our lives. If God had shown me the something better He had for me, it would no longer have required a faith response on my part. I would simply have been choosing the better path. Instead, God wanted me to trust that He had better plans for me, and to focus my eyes on Him . . . not the storm or the boat . . . and move forward. It took me a while and a little bit of wrestling before I was truly able to turn it over to God; but when I did, He began to shape my life in beautiful ways that

I could have never even imagined. He taught me to trust Him; and He took me into deeper relationship with Him, in which I began to discover purpose for my life on a whole new level. Then, less than a year later, He brought that "someone else" into my life . . . . the someone who has the same heart that God has given me, the someone who loves me for who I am, the someone who always has been part of God's beautiful plan for my life. That someone is now husband to me and father to our four precious children. God knew what He was doing all along; I just had to let go, trust Him, and allow Him to perfect His plan in me.

So many times we hold on to things because we are afraid of the unknown. We don't know what will happen if we let go, so we hold on to the familiar even when we know it is not God's plan for our lives. We say that we believe He knows best, but it's hard to really trust Him with everything we have and everything we are.

Remember that He created you, formed you, loves you and has a divine purpose for you. You can trust Him with your life . . . *ALL* of it.

God may be calling you to do something for Him and you're afraid to leave your boat of comfort. It can be scary to step out and do something for God. Many times God's plan for us calls us to face our fears. Maybe you have a fear of speaking in public, singing in front of a crowd, praying out loud, sharing your testimony, etc. Sometimes when God beckons us to do something, it is terrifying. Just know that in your weakness, He is strong. If He calls you to do it, He will strengthen you and enable you . . . but maybe not until that very moment that you step up to the plate. He is waiting for you to step out in faith . . . into the unknown, the scary, where you have to rely solely on Him . . . . and He will meet you there. God will never leave you hanging! When you put your faith in Him, be sure that He will show up. God doesn't use those vessels that feel capable and confident. If He did, they would boast in themselves. Instead, He chooses the vessels that declare, "I can't do it," "I'm not worthy," "I don't have what it takes" . . . because then His power can shine through.

When God called Moses to lead the Israelites out of Egypt, Moses' answer was, "Who am I that I should go to Pharaoh, and that I should bring the children of Israel out of Egypt?" (*Exodus 3:11 NKJV*) He later answered God, "O my Lord, I am not eloquent, neither before nor since You have spoken to Your servant; but I am slow of speech and slow of tongue." (*Exodus 4:10 NKJV*) I love God's answer! "So the Lord said to him, 'Who has made man's mouth? Or who makes the mute, the deaf, the seeing or the blind? Have not I, the Lord?

Now therefore, go, and I will be with your mouth and teach you what you shall say." (*Exodus 4:11-12 NKJV*) Somehow, this promise still wasn't enough for Moses, so God agreed to send Aaron as spokesperson for Moses. God used Moses in a mighty way, but I wonder how different the story might have been if Moses had trusted God to be "with his mouth." When God spoke to Moses from the burning bush, He was already fully aware of Moses' inabilities. He called him in spite of them.

Moses was not the only man called from nothingness to greatness. In the book of Judges, God raised up a warrior to deliver His people from the hands of the Midianites. He addressed Gideon as a "mighty warrior". (*Judges 6:12*) The Lord appeared to Gideon underneath a tree on his father's property and commanded, "Go in the strength you have and save Israel out of Midian's hand. Am I not sending you?" (*Judges 6:14 NIV*) Much like Moses, Gideon was well aware of his incapacities. He replied, "O my Lord, how can I save Israel? Indeed my clan is the weakest in Manasseh, and I am the least in my father's house." (*Judges 6:15 NKJV*) Again God chose a weak vessel to do his mighty work, so that His power could be displayed through him. Gideon recognized that he was unable to carry out his given task on his own. That realization caused him to rely completely on God's strength. It required complete faith that God would come through. God was trying to teach His people to lean on Him for their deliverance. To be sure that the children of Israel didn't become too confident in their own ability, God slimmed Gideon's army from over 30,000 men to 300 men. He uttered to Gideon, "The people who are with you are too many for me to give the Midianites into their hands, lest Israel claim glory for itself against me, saying, 'My own hand has saved me.'" *(Judges 7:2 NKJV)* When Gideon surrendered all that he had to God, God used him to bring deliverance to Israel against incredible odds. Gideon was right. He couldn't do it. But when He allowed God to work *through* him, the impossible was accomplished.

I could go on and on with Biblical accounts of weak, incompetent people whom God empowered to do mighty works for Him. David, the runt of his family, was victorious over the giant Goliath. Isaiah, who declared himself "a man of unclean lips", *(Isaiah 6:5)*, became the prophetic voice of God that told of the coming Messiah. Mary, who had never known a man, conceived and brought forth the son of God in flesh.

God is not limited by our weaknesses or inabilities. His greatness shines through them. Remember that "[His] grace is sufficient for you, for [his] strength is made perfect in weakness."(II *Corinthians 12:9 NKJV)* True faith in God requires us to step out on His strength in the absence of our own self-confidence. What can

God do through you if you turn your weaknesses and your inabilities over to Him? He wouldn't call you to it, if He didn't plan to meet you there and see you through it! Just step out of the boat.

CHAPTER 2

God's plan is unfolded
ONE STEP AT A TIME

Jaxsen is exactly one year and twenty-two days old today, and stubborn. Of our four children, he is the only one who wasn't walking before his first birthday. He's simply content crawling. I know, however, that any day he'll take his first step, and he'll quickly leave the crawling behind. That first step is his responsibility, his choice. Then nature will kick in, he'll see that it's all right, and he will walk.

Such a simple concept . . . one step. Yet that one step serves as the corridor for a great accomplishment. It marks the end of infancy and the beginning of toddlerhood. It gives so much freedom, yet is pre-empted by so much fear. It's a "step" into the unknown. What will happen? Will he fall? Yet the alternative is to continue crawling around on hands and knees. That would certainly get tiring and disgusting after a while.

As adults, we understand not only the significance of a first step, but the simplicity as well. Still when God calls us to take a spiritual step into the unknown, we often react much the same way as Jaxsen. We would rather continue crawling than face the dreaded fear of an unknown future. We settle in our comfort zones, though I'm not sure why we call them "comfort" zones. The truth is, once we've sensed God's calling to something different, something deeper, we can no longer be comfortable where we are.

Jaxsen doesn't know what will happen when he takes that first step, and he won't know until he takes it. In the same way, we cannot expect to know what will happen when we take our first step either . . . until we take it. We want God to hand us a completed plan with all the details of our lives following the "step", but God is asking us in faith to trust Him, one step at a time. The beauty of the lesson is taking each step as He leads it, with our hand in His. "The steps of a good man are ordered by the Lord." *(Psalm 37:23 KJV)*

Instead of trying to figure out how all the details will work out, celebrate the excitement of each step of faith. We need not worry how things will work out, because *"we know that in all things God works for the good of those who love him, who have been called according to His purpose." (Romans 8:28 NIV)*

When God called Abraham to go to Ur, he went. He didn't ask God how he'd be able to provide for himself and his family, whether he'd be welcomed, or even what he'd do once he arrived . . . He just went. Abraham knew that if God was leading him, everything would be all right. God wouldn't steer him wrong.

We won't always be able to figure out how God is intending to accomplish His purposes, but we must have faith that He has a plan—a good plan—for us and that He will fulfill it to completion. *(. . . he who began a good work in you will carry it on to completion until the day of Christ Jesus. Philippians 1:6 NIV)*

As I look back on my life, there were many instances in which God called me to take a step forward that was difficult. Each of those steps, however, was leading me to where I am in the Lord right now. I realize that there will be many more of those steps in my Christian journey; but if I'll continue to trust Him as He leads me step by step, His perfect plan will continue to unfold.

CHAPTER 3

Life is a JOURNEY, not a destination

"Life" = distance between birth and eternity. As someone once said, it's the dash on the tombstone. Too many people rush through life to find their way into the unreachable "future", only to get to the end and discover that the "life" they were searching for is now laying behind them as they stare in the face of an emptiness they've created by missing the many moments they should have treasured . . . the moments that would define them . . . the moments that make up their lives.

I loved the incomparable feeling of holding my newborn babies for the first time. Floods of emotion invaded my body, my mind, my whole being . . . every time. Four times experienced, it was equally amazing each time. Relief—that all was well, joy-to finally see the tiny person that we had named and talked to and so anxiously awaited, and love-unconceivable, overwhelming love for this new person. But what if that moment were cut short? What if the new little person instantly transformed into a mature adult? What if we missed all the other defining moments?

Seems a bit insane, huh? Yet somehow, we expect our lives to work like that. We want to instantaneously arrive at some designated destination in life, some place of complete fulfillment. The problem is—without the experiences that we gain on the way, we'd be empty and immature at that envisioned "destination." Those moments encountered on the journey define us . . . teach us.

We celebrate each child's first step, first words, first smile, first laugh, and first day of school. The joys of life are found in the small milestones along the way, and each one is a stepping stone in the path of the fulfillment of our higher calling.

When God calls us into some great purpose for Him, He calls us into a journey. We don't instantly arrive at some "final goal." My youth pastor once told me that a call to ministry is always a call to prepare.

God puts a longing in our heart . . . a purpose . . . then He begins making us into the person we need to be to fulfill that purpose. Each stage of the process is beautiful, a learning experience that draws us closer to God and enables us to become more like Him, taking on the desires of His heart.

On a quiet morning in October of 2004, I knew exactly what God was calling me to do. I'd been waiting on that moment for so long. As a junior high student, I had sensed God's calling to a deeper, more intimate relationship with Him. I had made a resolve to forego my afternoon TV ritual to seek God, studying His Word and praying for His guidance. I knew God was "calling" me, but I didn't know what He was calling me to do. I began to get discouraged as I neared the end of my high school years. Other young people in my youth group—who were younger than I—were announcing the particular callings God had revealed to them . . . but despite my seeking . . . I still didn't know what God was calling me to do. I didn't know where to go to college, what to major in, what my purpose was in life. Then, following a youth rally one night, someone spoke something to me that changed my life. Unaware of my internal struggle with God's calling on my life, He told me, "God is not so concerned with *what* He wants you to do as with *who* He wants you to be. Wow! God had been trying to mold me into a prepared vessel to honor Him. He'd been teaching me to seek Him, to trust Him . . . . filling me with His Word and His presence . . . and that was the primary calling He had for that time in my life. I began to seek God for the next step and tried to stop looking for the "complete plan." I made plans to attend a college that I now felt was God's direction, still unsure of a college major.

That morning in October, however, the wondering was satisfied . . . completely. As I gazed out the window of the BMDMI mission home in Managua, Nicaragua over the foggy landscape of the Central American country, I sensed, with everything within me, the calling to serve the country of Nicaragua as a full-time missionary. At that moment, nothing else mattered. My education seemed insignificant. "Home" took on a new meaning as the intents of my heart shifted drastically to the country and people of Nicaragua. I yearned to be there and to instantly begin the ministry that God had so clearly called me into . . . . But He said, "not yet" . . . Suddenly, I was awakened from my thoughts as a man sitting near me spoke to me. His name was Gus. He knew nothing about me except what he'd seen during our three days spent together at a BMDMI graduation event. But the words he spoke cut straight through the focus of my thoughts to my heart. He said, "Just do what God has you doing right now . . . and you never know how He will use you." It was as if God immediately confirmed through Gus what He'd just spoken to my spirit. Although He'd called me into the mission field, He had other plans for this particular part of my life. I had to wait, to learn, to grow. It is all part of the journey.

When we understand that God has called us, we have to understand that there is more to that calling than us perfecting a certain title or ministry. He is calling us into a deeper relationship with Him where He can develop and mold us into vessels that He can use.

CHAPTER 4

It's more about *WHO* God wants you to be than *WHAT* He wants you to do

I once read that God's calling for our lives is a "dual" calling, consisting primarily of the Christian call that God desires for every person to fulfill and, secondly, of the specified calling that God has for each individual. Therefore, before we can identify and fulfill our individual callings, we learn to live in that primary, Christian calling. What, then, is that primary calling? How do we discover God's calling for His special creation? Simple. We look in the Word.

When we search God's Word, I believe we find four distinct facets of who God is calling us to be as

Christians and how He expects us to live. He calls us to be servants, witnesses, worshippers and a holy people, set apart for Him.

Called to be servants

God's expectation for us to be servants is clearly exemplified in the person of Jesus Christ throughout His earthly ministry. Although He was God, He lived in humble fashion, never exalting Himself, but rather ministering to those no one else dared to even touch. Philippians 2:6-8 puts it this way:

> *[Jesus], who, being in very nature God, did not consider equality with God something to be grapsed, but made himself nothing, taking the very nature of a servant, being made in human likeness. And being found in appearance as a man, he humbled himself and became obedient to death—even death on a cross! (NIV)*

He knew who He was . . . but He was on a mission that was more important to Him than attaining any kind of earthly glory. We are to be servants committed to the mission of God, serving Him first, and then those to whom He has sent us.

What, then, is a servant?

If you've been out to eat lately, then you know what it means to have a good "server" or waiter. Waiters portray good examples of servant-hood. A good waiter will constantly check on his customer to ensure that his needs are being completely met. The waiter does not focus on himself . . . but on those whom he is serving. The waiter may or may not receive a tip, but if he's a good waiter, he will do his best without expecting a tip. (Although giving a tip is certainly the gracious thing to do!)

In the same way, we should serve others expecting nothing in return. It's our "job" as Christians. Jesus said in a parable, "Will [the master] thank the servant because he did what he was told to do? So you also, when you have done everything you were told to do, should say, 'We are unworthy servants; we have only done our duty.'" *(Luke 17:9-10 NIV)*

"Servant" denotes a low (humble) position. Servants should serve as if the ones being served are more important than themselves. This doesn't mean we think of ourselves as worthless. We are all equally important in God's eyes . . . but we should treat others more highly than ourselves. *(Do nothing out of selfish ambition or vain conceit, but in humility consider others better than yourselves. Phil 2:3 NIV)*

So important is our calling to servant-hood that is was one of the last lessons Jesus taught His disciples before finishing His earthly ministry. At the last supper on the night of His arrest, Jesus knelt down and began to wash His disciples' feet. In doing so, He was taking on the job of a lowly servant. When He finished, He commissioned them to "do as I have done to you." (*John 13:15 NIV*)

Although the story of Jesus washing the disciples' feet has always been a favorite of mine, I began to see it in a brand new light one summer outside the makeshift kitchen of our mission team in a small village in Nicaragua. I had showered in our metal shower stall late the night before, but the constant daily rain showers had created a muddy frosting on the tall grass that lined the pathway to the kitchen. By the time I made it to the top of the hill in my flip-flops, I had a slick brown coating of mud on my feet. I wasn't particularly concerned, since we were gearing up for a day's work in the muddy streets anyway. A few of my team members joked about my dirty feet, and I laughed along . . . . But our team leader proceeded to do something I would have never imagined.

Our team leader, Mr. Binnie Turnage, is one of the most precious people I have ever known. Although he is in his seventies, he still travels faithfully to Nicaragua at least once a year to serve as leader of an evangelical-medical mission team. If anyone has a reason to be boastful, it's Brother Binnie. He's a man of outstanding character and worldly success, but he is noted for his utter humility. I have never seen so much of the love of Christ in any one person as I see in Mr. Binnie.

At the sight of my nasty feet that day, he walked over to the table outside the kitchen and tore off a paper towel. He dipped it into a barrel of rainwater, knelt down, and began to scrub the filth off my feet. I just stood there . . . frozen in humility, broken in gratitude. A moment's glimpse at two other members of my team who were standing nearby assured me they were thinking the same thing I was thinking . . . Peter. I now felt sure that I was experiencing a little of what he must have felt when Jesus knelt to wash his feet. I, too, wanted to say, "No! Get up, you can't do that," but I knew that all I could do was stand there, treasure the moment, commit it to memory, and "do likewise."

The true picture of servant-hood is the surrender of yourself in an attempt to minister to others the love and compassion of Jesus Christ. We can't be afraid to get dirty. We cannot consider ourselves "above" service. Instead we should humble ourselves and serve from our hearts in an attempt to demonstrate the love of Christ to a needy world.

Called to be witnesses

Our commission doesn't stop with a call to minister to the hurting. The greatest service we could do for anyone is to share with them the Good News of Jesus Christ. We are called to be witnesses.

When Jesus was getting ready to leave His disciples, He passed His ministry on to them . . . to us. He declared,

> *"As the Father has sent me, I am sending you." (John 20:21 NIV)*
> "Witness" is not merely something we're called to *do*; it is *who* we're called to *be*. (*But you shall receive power when the Holy Spirit has come upon you; and you shall be witnesses to me in Jerusalem, and in all Judea and Samaria, and to the end of the earth. Acts 1:8 NKJV*)

Where are we called to witness?

Wherever we are . . . in the school that we attend, the job that we hold, the household we live in . . . wherever God has placed us during this season of our lives is the field where He intends for us to sow the seeds of His Gospel. Often we think that going door to door, serving in a soup kitchen, or taking part in a mission trip is the way to witness to others about

Jesus Christ. While all of these avenues are good, and I believe, essential; witnessing cannot be confined to such instances. We witness with our words, and we witness with our lives everywhere we go and in everything that we say. We should live lives that testify to the goodness and grace of Jesus, and take advantage of every opportunity to share the Good News of the Gospel with others.

Who are we supposed to witness to?

Everyone. We cannot choose who we believe is deserving of the Gospel or who we believe is ready to accept. Would you have chosen Paul, a religious zealot who made killing the followers of Jesus his life's ambition? Matthew, an upper-class thief? Peter, a hot-headed fisherman? Mary Magdalene, a prostitute? Sometimes those we would deem "unworthy" are the very ones Jesus has purposefully placed in our path to be the recipients of our ministry.

After Saul's conversion on the road to Damascus, the Lord spoke to Ananias and sent him to go and minister to Saul. Ananias was afraid and unwilling at first because he knew Saul's past. He must have thought, "Surely, Lord, You're mistaken." But the Lord told Ananias, "Go, for he is a chosen vessel of mine to bear my name before Gentiles, kings, and the children of Israel. For I will show him how many things he must suffer for my name's sake." *(Acts 9:15-16 NKJV)* Man sees outward appearance, but God looks at the heart; *(I Samuel 16:7)* and He sees potential.

I recently attended job training with my husband in New Orleans, Louisiana. We thought it would be a nice get-away. He would go to class during the day while I rested, then we could spend time together in the evenings. As we neared the hotel, however, we changed our minds about exploring outside the perimeter of the hotel. We were in the heart of downtown New Orleans, about one street away from the infamous Bourbon Street. I'm a small town girl, and I'd only heard about the things that go on around Bourbon Street. Driving up to our hotel at eleven o'clock that night, I was assured that everything I'd heard was absolutely true. As I watched people on the sidewalks, my reactions were varied. From some, I quickly turned my head. At the sight of others, I couldn't help but laugh at the absurdity of their appearance. Needless to say, I wanted to get away from all of them . . . fast. Later that night, as I was lying in the bed, I felt remorseful for my attitude. I realized that in turning my head, I was judging those people. Not only judging them, but writing them off as doomed people. That is NOT the way Christ would have responded. I'm not sure what I could have said or done for any of those people that night, but I do know that the attitude of my heart was wrong. Instead of judging, I should have felt pity and compassion. A Christ-like heart would hurt for them and seek to minister His grace and truth to them. I could have at least offered a warm smile and a non-judging glance. I asked God to change my heart so that I could see people the way He sees them. After all, when He was accused of hanging out with the sinners . . . the prostitutes . . . the dirty . . . the filth of society, He responded, "Those who are well have no need of a physician, but those who are sick. I have not come to call the righteous, but sinners, to repentance." (Luke 5:31-32 NKJV)

In order to be witnesses, we must first take on the heart of God and His desire that none should perish but that all should come to repentance. *(II Peter 3:9)* We ought to live in such a way that others see the light and love of Christ in our lives . . . And we should always be ready to take advantage of an opportunity to share Christ with others. Peter tells us to "Always be prepared to give an answer to everyone who asks you to give the reason for the hope that you have."(I *Peter 3:15 NIV)*

When should we be witnesses?

Now! Jesus says in John 4:35, "Do you not say, 'Four months more and then the harvest'? I tell you, open your eyes and look at the fields! They are ripe for harvest." *(NIV)* The time to share the gospel of Jesus Christ with our families, our neighbors, our world—is now. Ephesians 5:16 says we should live "making the most of every opportunity." *(NIV)*

Just as Esther was placed in the kingdom of Xerxes "for such a time as this", *(Esther 4:14 NIV)* we are part of this generation for *this* time—*this* moment. Life is fleeting. Use every moment wisely. Take advantage of every opportunity to lead someone else to Christ.

We are called to be worshippers.

All of creation exists by God and for His glory. Every minute detail of creation brings glory to God. We are no exception. We were created to bring glory to our Creator . . . . that is . . . . to worship Him. Humans are born with an instinctive drive to worship. Open any history book and you'll find that a very important part of the culture of any tribe or group is their religion . . . who or what they worship. Some have worshipped idols. Others have worshipped nature itself. Many worship unseen forces or gods. Regardless of the target of their worship, all people groups have sought out something or someone to worship. That fact alone should substantiate the claim that we are created to worship. Objects of worship have changed a little bit in our society. Often our objects of worship are people, sports or maybe our empire of wealth. Sometimes, we focus our worship on rituals or religions themselves. Still, the intended target of our worship is our Creator, God himself.

In recent years, we have coined the term "praise and worship" to describe the part of our service in which we sing (usually contemporary 'praise and worship' songs), but this label greatly diminishes our understanding of true worship. Worship is about so much more than singing songs that give us a certain "feeling" or emotional stirring. Worship is our spirit responding to the greatness of God. It's our realization of how great He is and how insignificant we are. True worship begins deep within our soul and radiates through our entire being.

Worship isn't restricted to a time when we are alone in the presence of God, but it is an ongoing part of our lives. The very breath we breathe, when exhaled in gratitude brings glory to our Creator and can be an expression of worship. When we take worship off our list of duties and make it part of our character description, it will become something we can do in even the most menial tasks of our lives. Romans 12:1 says, "Therefore, I urge you, brothers, in view of God's mercy, to offer your bodies as a living sacrifice, holy and pleasing to God—this is your spiritual act of worship." *(NIV)* Worship begins when we consecrate our lives to God and ask Him to be glorified in every part of our lives and bodies.

When Jesus was talking with the woman at the well, she asked Him to enlighten her on the correct place to worship. Apparently, the people were disputing the correct means of carrying out their religious rituals. Jesus disclosed to her that the Father wasn't concerned with such rituals. He told her that they didn't even know what they were worshipping. They had gotten so entangled in their religious practices that they forgot about the true object of their worship . . . God. He then expressed to her, "God is spirit, and those who worship Him must worship in spirit and truth." *(John 4:24 NKJV)*

To worship God **in spirit** is to worship Him from our inmost being, from the most profound parts of who we are . . . . to give Him everything. The Spanish word for "to worship" is *adorar*. This word is also a way of expressing love . . . the deepest kind of love. When we think of the person we love the most—a parent, a spouse, a child—our love is beyond description. "I love you" is much more than an expression we use to convey an emotion. We love with all that we are, beyond expression. We would do anything for that person. We'd give our lives to show our love. This is the significance of the word *adorar* . . . . and this should be the extent to which we relay our worship to God. We should give everything that is within us, everything that we are to show our absolute love and adoration for Him . . . . everywhere and at all times. When we worship in spirit, worship becomes an inherent song that forever extends from our very souls.

To worship **in truth** means that we understand Who it is that we worship and why we worship. We do not worship because someone is singing our favorite song. We do not worship because our parents taught us that we should take part in these religious ceremonies. We do not worship because everyone else is doing it. We worship because we recognize that God is God, that He is our Creator, our Father, the Forgiver of our sins, the King of Kings, the Lord of Lords, and that He is absolutely worthy. And we worship because we love Him. When Isaiah stood in the presence of Almighty God, he saw God for who He is and he saw himself for who he was. He exclaimed, "Woe is me, for I am undone! Because I am a man of unclean lips, and I dwell in the midst of a people of unclean lips; for my eyes have seen the King, the Lord of hosts." (Isaiah 6:5 *NKJV*) In the very presence of God, he saw God in all His holiness and realized just how sinful he himself was. His response was absolute worship. When we see God for who He is and recognize that we are nothing in comparison with Him, we can worship Him in truth.

In the book of Isaiah, the Lord rebuked his people for their "fake" worship. The Lord says: "These people come near to me with their mouth and honor me with their lips, but their hearts are far from me. Their worship of me is made up only of rules taught by men". *(Isaiah 29:13 NIV)* Although they were doing all the right things on the outside, their hearts were not bearing true worship to God. He continues in verse 23, "When they see among them their children, the work of my hands, they will keep my name holy; they will acknowledge the holiness of the Holy One of Jacob, and will stand in awe of the God of Israel." The true worship that God desired from Israel was that they reverence His holiness and stand in awe of Him.

You don't have to be able to sing or play a musical instrument to offer worship to the Lord. When we truly worship, we will recognize the greatness of God, reverence His holiness, and respond with all we have in whatever manner we can to express to Him our love, our awe and our adoration. Our entire life will resound with adulation. THAT is what it means to be a worshipper.

We are called to be holy

Regardless of what occupation we choose, where we choose to live, where we attend school, etc., we are called to be holy, set apart for God's use. When we ask Jesus Christ to be Lord of our lives, we are committing to a life surrendered totally to Him. Before we make all the other decisions about how to best follow His will, is it essential that we decide to live holy lives.

Peter reminds us in I Peter 2:9 that we are a "holy nation", called into light from darkness. A little earlier in I Peter 1:15, he instructs us to "be holy, as He who has called you is holy." Remember that the word "Christian" means "little Christ." If we call ourselves Christians, we should reflect the image of our Lord Jesus Christ, which is a holy image. While we live in a world filled with sin, we are to be different. We should shine as "lights in the darkness".

According to II Corinthians 6:17, we should come out from among the [world] and be separate. Our lives should mark stark contrast to the unholy lifestyle exemplified by the world around us. Unless we let our lives shine with godliness, we will blend into the darkness. Paul urges the Christians of Rome, "do not be conformed to this world, but be transformed by the renewing of your mind, that you may prove what is that good and acceptable and perfect will of God." *(Romans 12:2 NKJV)*

If we want to discover the perfect will of God for our lives, we must first become consecrated to Him, set apart from this world and dedicated to His Kingdom. If we seek after His heart, He will share with us the heart and mind of Christ.

What does it mean to be holy?

To be holy is to be "without spot or blemish". We live in a sinful world, and we're bound to get our feet dirty as we walk through the filth. We must, however, allow God's blood to cleanse us from all unrighteousness and seek daily to crucify the lusts of the flesh. Paul advises us, "Walk in the Spirit, and ye shall not fulfill the lust of the flesh." *(Galatians 5:16 KJV)* The key, then, is to set our minds on spiritual things rather than on things of this world. The Bible assures us that, although we live *in* this world, we do not have to be *of* this world. *(John 15:19)* We have to dedicate ourselves to a holy standard of living. While some of those standards are explicitly set forth for us in Scripture, some of them have to be sought out through our personal relationship with Jesus Christ. When we seek to represent Jesus Christ and to live in a way that will testify to His glory, we will be able to approach a holy lifestyle.

Paul advised young Timothy in I Timothy 4:12 to set an example with his life in speech, in life, in love, in faith and in purity. When we consecrate every part of our lives to God, we can truly be effective ambassadors for Jesus; and we'll be tuned in to His voice as He directs our paths.

I was recently reminded by a dear friend that if we cannot relate our lives and ministry to the life and ministry of Christ, then we need to step back and take a closer look at our motives and ambitions. It is possible to become so focused on the "will of Christ" that we forget to seek the "heart of Christ". I've heard it said that sometimes we put all our thoughts and efforts into the work of the Lord until we forget to focus on the Lord of the work. Seek God's heart, not just His plan, and He'll reveal both to you.

It's not so much about choosing the perfect college major, the perfect career, or even the "right" ministry. It's about being *who* God wants you to be in whatever path He is leading you in this season of your life. Your goals may change. Your career may change. Your situations may change. Sometimes God leads you into different places in different phases of your Christian journey. Through it all, strive to be obedient and to live your life set apart and consecrated to the Lord.

"Trust in the Lord with all your heart and lean not on your own understanding. In all your ways acknowledge Him, and He will make your paths straight." (*Proverbs 3:5-6 NIV*)

CHAPTER 5

If you don't pass the test,
you will be RETESTED

As a teacher, I understand that a student cannot advance to the next level until he has mastered the current level of study. In order to determine whether the student has really learned the lesson, he is tested.

The same is true in our spiritual growth. God teaches, then He tests us to see if we have truly grasped that thing He was teaching. Until we pass the test, we cannot move forward.

Many times we find ourselves dealing with the same exasperating trials over and over again and we wonder why we can't seem to get a break. Perhaps God is trying to teach us something. Perhaps we have failed the test and are being re-tested, given another chance to learn an important life lesson. Now, by saying that perhaps you've failed the test, I'm not saying that you've failed God or sinned. I am simply implying that you may have failed to truly trust God in your situation. Sometimes we say that we trust Him after He has brought us through, only because we are no longer in the heat of the trial. Then, when presented with a similar trial, we see that we don't really trust Him like we should.

I know that I have found myself facing the same hurdles repeatedly on several occasions. Then, when I'd stop and look back, I'd see that God was trying to teach me to let go and trust Him, that He will always provide, that He is faithful.

For years, my husband and I bounced back and forth from "financially sound" to "scraping by." It seemed as if every time we thought we had everything under control, the rug was yanked from under our feet. Shane lost his job, had to have unexpected knee surgery, etc. Each time something like this happened, I became the queen of stress, letting my worry transform me into a grouchy, emotional wreck . . . and each time, God took care of us. He always provided for the bills to be paid. He always put food on our table. Yet the next time we faced a similar trial, I found myself reacting with stress and doubt all over again.

Each time the storm was over, I declared God faithful and trustworthy, but when the clouds darkened overhead again and the bank account began to empty, I seemed to forget what God had taught me. So . . . He continued to re-test us. I eventually began to see the pattern and realized that God was waiting for us to trust Him *in* the storm, not *after* the storm.

Well, those dark clouds began to roll in again a few weeks ago. My husband works offshore, so he spends three weeks at home and three weeks at work. The day he was scheduled to return to work, he woke up with a pain in his leg. Throughout the day, the pain worsened. We didn't take it seriously, because he didn't think he had injured it in any way. By the time he drove the five hour, overnight drive to Louisiana to catch his helicopter to work, however, he couldn't even walk due to the severity of the pain. His supervisor sent him home to go to the doctor and determine the problem. I was worried. He really needed to be at work. His doctor visit the following day revealed a pulled muscle—nothing serious but he would miss an entire week of work.

Shane gently reminded me that everything was going to be alright—that God had this situation under control. He was right; so together, we decided to trust Him.

When a week had passed, Shane faxed in his release to return to work and began to pack for the trip. A phone call that afternoon, however, redirected our plans again. They already had a full crew scheduled to fly on the helicopter and would not have room for Shane for another five days. This time, it was Shane whom I found lying on our bed, staring at the ceiling with a look of concern on his face. Now it was my turn. A decision had to be made . . . worry, and start asking the "What do we do now?" questions . . . or trust God. We would trust God. I reminded Shane as he'd reminded me a few days earlier to trust God. Again we chose faith over fear and doubt. Although the problem was still present, the burdens were lifted when we turned them over to God . . . And God came through. It was only a couple of hours later when Shane received the phone call that they'd made room for him on the helicopter and that he could return to work after all! And the blessings had only begun.

The helicopter had only flown about fifteen minutes from the port when autopilot failed and they had to return to the heliport. The flight was postponed for the following day. The minute Shane boarded the ship the next day, people began to congratulate him, though he had no idea why. When he spoke with his supervisors, he learned that he had been promoted! The position he'd been training for came open . . . that very morning. God's timing to get him back to the ship was *perfect*. The situation that we thought was going to be a bleak trial became an awesome blessing.

Remember that, in order to have a testimony, you must endure a test. Trust God. He is faithful to bring you through. He desires that we learn to trust Him in those situations that are hardest for us to surrender; whether in our finances, our family, our health or any other trying circumstances we face. We, like Job, may have trouble finding God in the middle of the test, but remember, the teacher is always silent during the test. *(But if I go to the east, he is not there; if I go to the west, I do not find him. When he is at work in the north, I do not see him; when he turns to the south, I catch no glimpse of him. Job 23:8-9)* He's still right there with us. *(But he knows the way that I take; when he has tested me, I will come forth as gold. Job 23:10)* He knows right where you are and understands what you are going through. He promised never to put more on us than we can bear. *(I Cor. 10:13)* So trust Him, and pass the test!

CHAPTER 6

God will give you all you need to do what He calls you to do

Delight yourself in the Lord, and he will give you the desires of your heart. Ps. 37:4 NIV

And my God will meet all your needs according to his glorious riches in Christ Jesus. Phil. 4:19 NIV

S o many times I have found myself wondering why I can't do something as well as someone else. I must admit that I have often been jealous of someone else's ability to do something better than I. I have wondered why someone who begins to do something I've done for much longer seems to progress beyond my ability so quickly.

For example, I have been playing keyboard for several years now. I have improved a lot through the years, but I have seen others start playing below my ability and advance beyond it in a few months' time. I have been very frustrated by such instances. However, God has taught me that His plan for those people may rely heavily upon these talents, while His plan for me is something totally different. He uses my ability to play the keyboard, but His calling on my life is foreign mission work. Therefore, while I may use my ability in my calling, it is not the main focus. God has given me sufficient ability on the keyboard to use for what He intends for me to do. Instead of questioning why I do not possess the same talents as someone else, I need only to use what God has given me to the best of my ability to glorify Him fully. After all, it's not about me! If He calls me to be a concert pianist, He'll increase my ability! (Although, I seriously doubt that will ever happen.)

God increases my ability as the place of my calling changes. Since taking on the ministry of worship leader in my church, He's given me better singing and playing ability than I've ever had. I have grown more in the last few months than I had in several years combined. God is making me the singer and musician I need to be in order to please Him as worship leader. Before I served in this position, I didn't need that ability as much. I know now that God will make sure that my abilities and talents are sufficient to serve wherever He needs me to serve if I'll only be willing to turn over all that I have to Him, no matter how small or insignificant it may seem.

I have often heard it said that God doesn't call the qualified, He qualifies the called. God doesn't take what abilities we have and give us a calling that fits them; He calls us and then gives us whatever we need to fulfill that calling. Instead of focusing our thoughts on what we *can't* do, we should focus our energy on giving what we *can* do to God to be used for His glory.

I have often felt that I do a lot of things "ok", but nothing "great." Perhaps that is because God wants to use me in several places. I once had a youth pastor who put it well. He said that his calling was to be "caulk." He was called to fill in wherever needed. He didn't see himself as having one specific calling. Instead, he was the man God could use wherever there was something to be done or a hole to be filled. I like that concept. We need to be ready and willing to be used wherever God needs us at any given time. We don't have to be great at anything; we just have to be willing to be used in any way needed. God has had to remind me many times that no matter how well I do something, someone does it better . . . and that's ok! Ministry is **not** a competition. It's quite the opposite. It's a service. We must all work together and complement each other's abilities for the furtherance of the Kingdom of Christ.

When I wonder now why I can't seem to play, sing, teach, etc. as well as someone else, I gently remind myself that when God needs me to play, sing or teach that well, He will give me the ability to do so. Until then, my ability is perfectly what He needs it to be for me to fulfill the calling that I have on my life.

I read a Facebook post from a great friend of mine that really touched my heart. She is currently serving as a missionary teacher in Managua, Nicaragua. Each week she posts a list of things that she has learned that week. Number 7 on her list last week was, "I have learned that . . . when I made myself available to God and stopped looking to get credit, He started opening one door after another for me." I have watched her life as God has opened these doors for her, and I know the deep truth of this comment. My goal is to also be available to God totally for His glory. He can use this vessel, equip this vessel, and receive all the credit for the work that He has done in me and through me! Let Him do the same in you.

CHAPTER 7

When it comes down to it, all you really need is God

S ometimes God requires us to give Him what we desire most deeply in order to show us how much greater His plan is for our lives. I once heard it said, "Write your plans in pencil, but give God the eraser." It's wise to make plans for our lives. Otherwise, we'd be foolishly acting with no direction. However, if we want to live in the fullness of His will, we must be willing to submit our plans to God and allow Him to make changes when necessary. Often, things occur in our lives that we don't understand. Loss can be a very difficult thing. It comes in two different ways. Sometimes, things are taken from us outside of our control . . . and sometimes, we are asked to give things up of our own volition. Both types of loss can hurt deeply and leave us with an empty feeling inside.

We need to realize that where there are empty places in our lives, there are opportunities for us to be filled more fully with God's presence. He specializes in filling the empty places. Our lives will be full of something. Sometimes God asks us to empty ourselves of certain things so that He can fill those areas of our lives with better things. Sometimes, life just happens and emptiness occurs, such as in the case of untimely deaths, divorce/abandonment, etc. Even in these instances, however, God can fill the holes with so much more than we could ever imagine.

When God asks you to surrender your prize

God desires that we trust Him wholeheartedly with our lives. After all, He created us and designed our inmost being. *(For you created my inmost being; you knit me together in my mother's womb. Ps. 139:13 NIV) He* knows what His ultimate plan is for our lives; therefore, He knows the things that will bring us true fulfillment. Since we can only see from our mere human perspective, that is very difficult for us to understand. We are very emotional beings, and we react based on how we feel and what we can see "right now" in our lives. Sometimes, though, God asks us to hand over our most prized plans, possessions or even relationships in order to make room in our lives for something much better that He has in store for us. These situations **always** require a sacrifice, but we will **never** be disappointed if we trust Him. We need to remember that every good gift is from God, *(Every good and perfect gift is from above, coming down from the Father of the heavenly lights, who does not change like shifting shadows. James 1:17 NIV)*, and that all we have already belongs to Him anyway. We have to trust Him completely with everything and be willing to surrender it all to Him, knowing that He will withhold no good thing from His children. *(No good thing does he withhold from those whose walk is blameless. Psalm 84:11 NIV)*

A great example of such a required sacrifice can be found in the story of Abraham and Isaac. Abraham had prayed for a son; and in his old age, through a promise from God, he was blessed with Isaac. I can only imagine how precious this son was to him. Not only was Isaac Abraham and Sarah's only son, he was a miracle and the avenue of the promised future blessings of God on Abraham's descendants. Yet God asked him to sacrifice Isaac on the altar as an act of worship. Abraham must have been devastated, afraid and certainly confused. How could God take this blessing back from him?

How could God ever fulfill his promise to Abraham if he took the heir of that promise? But Abraham trusted God. He knew that God had blessed him with this son against all hope or reason, and he knew that God would continue to be faithful to His promise to him. He loved and trusted God enough to let go of the most precious thing in his life at God's request. And God honored Abraham's sacrifice. He did not require Isaac's life. He provided a ram, and He kept his promise to Abraham. Abraham was blessed because of his faithfulness and his sacrifice. Although Abraham did not take Isaac's life, the sacrifice had already occurred in his heart when he obediently headed to Mt. Moriah with his son. Because He did not hold back anything from God, God blessed him abundantly and made him the Father of many nations.

When I was very young, my daddy read a story to me that has lingered in my mind throughout the years. It was the story of a little girl, her daddy and a string of fake pearls. Her daddy had given her the pearls as a gift and she treasured them more than anything in the world. She wore them everywhere. One night, her daddy came to tuck her in and asked, "Do you love me?" The little girl replied, "Oh yes, Daddy, you know I love you." In response her daddy replied, "Then give me your pearls." She said, "Oh, no Daddy, not my pearls." She offered to give him any other toy except those prized pearls. Her daddy simply said, "That's okay." and kissed her goodnight. A few nights later he returned with the same request only to hear the little girl pleading again for him to take anything but the pearls. The next night when he came to tuck her in, he found her on her bed in tears. She held out her hand and said, "Here Daddy, you can have my pearls." He took the pearls, reached in his pocket and handed the little girl a small box. She opened it to find a strand of real pearls inside.

Only when she was willing to surrender the thing most precious to her did her father give her something much better that he'd been waiting to give her all along. She thought the fake pearls were a treasure, but her daddy gave her something far more valuable. In the same way, God often desires to give us great gifts, but He wants us to surrender our feeble treasures to Him first. He desires to see that we love the Giver more than the gifts and that we trust Him with those things that we treasure most.

If God asks you to hand something over to Him, trust Him completely and release it to Him. Every blessing you have has come from Him, and if He requires those blessings of you, then He will surely give you something greater in return.

When loss is inevitable

Because we live in a fallen world; pain, heartache, and even death are inevitable parts of life. We will face times of extreme sorrow that create indescribable emptiness in our lives. I have learned that God is enough to fill every empty spot if we will only let Him be.

My hero in this life was my daddy. I was as much of a "daddy's girl" as anyone could ever imagine. As a little girl, I rode the lawn mower with Daddy; I went to work with Daddy; I went to classic car shows with Daddy; I sat in Daddy's lap every night after supper to watch TV. As I grew older, the bond with my daddy never faded. He took me to school and walked me to my class through my sixth grade year. Unlike many young girls, I was never embarrassed to be daddy's little girl. I didn't care how old I was or what anyone else might think. He was my daddy and I was proud of it. I wrote him a poem for Father's Day in 2002, the summer before my senior year in high school, telling him what he meant to me. I wrote of my thankfulness for his godly guidance and his unmatched love for his family. I didn't realize at the time how timely and significant the poem would be.

Later that year, as I was coming home from school one Wednesday afternoon, I met an ambulance headed under the red light. I said my usual, "God bless them" prayer and continued on my way home, never imagining how my life was about to change. About five miles later, when I topped the hill to turn in my driveway, I saw the ambulance again. It was stopped now, at the bottom of my yard; and my daddy's 1929 Mercedes kit car was there in the ditch, completely demolished. Fear, pain, and a flutter of other emotions welled up inside me as I pulled over on the side of the road and rushed out of my own car. I ran across the road searching frantically for a sign of my daddy. A cousin of mine who worked next door at the Forestry Commission had come to the scene. He grabbed me and refused to let me get any nearer to the accident. I tried desperately to get out of his grasp, crying, "He's my daddy!" My cousin assured me that he was going to be alright, but I knew that was not necessarily true. Since he wouldn't let go though, I had no choice but to let go. I cried out to God, and he heard me. I felt God's arms wrap around me as tangibly as my cousin's arms were wrapped around me, and my spirit was settled. I will not say that the next two hours were easy. We rushed to the emergency room where doctors worked busily, and we had no idea exactly what his condition was.

Because my daddy was a well-loved and upstanding Christian man of the community, a large crowd of people had gathered outside the emergency room waiting on an update on his condition. Somehow, God gave me the strength to visit with them, reassuring them that this situation was in God's hands. My constant subconscious prayer was, "Lord, please don't take my daddy; but if you do, please give me the strength to handle it." I asked the group of people gathered outside to please make a circle so that we could pray. As we said, "Amen," my brother-in-law walked outside to let me know the doctors had begun performing CPR. Moments later, the doctor called us in to inform us that "His heart just wasn't strong enough." He was gone. Although my heart fell, I instantly felt God's presence begin to fill up the hole in my life. God allowed me to see that Daddy had lived a life full of love and purpose. Although it was cut short, he left behind a great godly legacy . . . Now I had to do the same. That day I truly learned what it means to call God "Father" and to experience a peace beyond my understanding. The pain was real, but God was more real.

Sometimes, we have to face great losses that seem as if they will drain every bit of life that is in us and leave us empty and void of any reason to continue living. I have learned that . . . even in these most desperate situations . . . God is enough. The pain will still come, but God will be all that we need to endure it and to find strength in the midst of our hurting. I have heard it said that when God is all you have, you can rest assured God is all you need. When you find yourself at the end of your rope, there you will find God, waiting to lift you up and carry you through your toughest times.

It is hard to understand why tragedies occur in our lives, especially those that seem so untimely. It is also hard to understand why we must sometimes surrender our plans, our dreams or our relationships, feeling as if we're leaving part of ourselves behind. We must remember that God's ways are so much higher than ours. *("For my thoughts are not your thoughts, neither are your ways my ways," declares the LORD. 'As the heavens are higher than the earth, so are my ways higher than your ways and my thoughts than your thoughts.'" Isaiah 55:8-9 NIV)* I like to think of life as a puzzle. We often cannot understand how all the pieces are supposed to fit together, but God is holding the box with the big picture. He knows perfectly how to put it all together to make the beautiful picture He designed our lives to be. Seek His will and trust him, remembering that "In all things God works for the good of those who love him, who have been called according to his purpose." *(Romans 8:28 NIV)*

CHAPTER 8

God is the only thing that can never be shaken

"Whoever comes to me and hears my sayings and does them, I will show you whom he is like: he is like a man building a house, who dug deep and laid the foundation on the rock; And when the flood arose, the stream beat vehemently against that house and could not shake it, for it was founded on the rock. But he who heard and did nothing is like a man who built a house on the earth without a foundation, against which the stream beat vehemently; and immediately it fell. And the ruin of that house was great."
Luke 6:47-49 NKJV

When the storms come, we must be standing on the Rock. This passage took on an all new meaning for me in the fall of 2004, when my friend Sharon and I stepped out of a truck on the top of a scenic overlook at Catarina, Nicaragua. The overlook is a popular tourist destination overlooking the Apoyo lagoon. We had visited the area before, but this time was different. As soon as we stepped out of the truck, we noticed a slight trembling of the ground. Unsure what to think at first, reality soon began to set in as we heard the murmurs around us . . . earthquake! The trembling grew stronger for only a few seconds, then died down. It was only a tremor from an earthquake near the coastline. No harm done. Those few seconds, however, seemed to put my life on pause—short-lived—yet long enough to let this eternal principle set in. My life must be founded on the Rock.

Everything else in life can be shaken . . . even the surest things in our lives, like the very ground under our feet. When it's all shaken, where will you be standing? Sometimes we base all our hope, trust and effort in our finances, our job, or even in certain people. Then, when they fail us, we don't know what to do or where to turn. We have nothing left, because our lives were built on shifting sand . . . on earthly treasures that rust and decay.

As Sharon grabbed my arm and gave me a wild-eyed "what do we do now" look, my mind began to race. I'm from Mississippi and she's from Tennessee, so this was our first earthquake experience. We have tornadoes in Mississippi, and we look for shelter in the lowest elevations. We have hurricanes, but we have sufficient warning to evacuate coastal areas. But where do you go when the ground is shaking . . . and possibly about to break? There is ultimately nowhere to go. Sure, some places have "earthquake resistant" buildings, but even they can only stand so much. I realized in that instant the importance of the simple truth of being built upon the Rock. No matter what happens in our lives, physical or otherwise, we have the Rock underneath us . . . the firm foundation . . . the God who does not shift or break. When everything else seems to crumble, He's still there, holding us . . . sustaining us.

Things—all things—are temporary. They all get old, wear out, decay. Situations are . . . well . . . situational. They change—constantly. People are human. They fail us. They will not always be there. "But Jesus Christ is the same yesterday, today and forever." *(Hebrews 13: 8 NKJV)* He will never leave or forsake us. *(Hebrews 13:5)* He is our refuge and our fortress in time of trouble. (Psalm *46:1)* Let your life be founded on Him.

CHAPTER 9

God doesn't have deadlines or limits

When He speaks, trust Him. He can open doors that no man can shut. Rev 3:8

How often are we frustrated by life's impossibilities, worried about things outside of our control? We want to follow God's will for our lives. We start off excited, like someone on an exciting road trip, ready for great adventure, ready to do great things for God. We feel unstoppable. Then . . . we see it "Road Closed 1500 feet ahead." We stop, discouraged, and turn around feeling that, somewhere, somehow, we've missed it. If we were really heading in the right direction, following God's call, this wouldn't have happened . . . right?

Well, let's think about it. How easy was the trek to Calvary as Jesus followed His Father's perfect will? He faced obstacles of pain, ridicule, slander and ultimately, death; but that didn't stop Him. He knew His mission, and He didn't stop until He'd declared it "finished." Rarely are our obstacles so harsh, but we can be sure we will face obstacles. We have to remember that He does not leave us alone on our journey, but is with us every step of the way *(. . . "I will never leave you nor forsake you." Hebrews 13:5 NKJV)*, and we will continually have to rely on Him, not on our own strength. *("Not by might, nor by power, but by my Spirit, says the Lord Almighty." Zechariah 4:6 NIV)*

Because we live in a world bound by limits, it is easy for us to take our eyes off the goal and become fixed on those limits. We can be restrained by deadlines, financial deficits, difficulties, or even insufficiencies of our own talents, abilities or strength.

If God calls you to do it; just get to it! Trust Him to guide you through the roadblocks. He is not bound by the limitations of this world. "What is impossible with man is possible with God." *(Luke 18:27 NIV)*

Just think of Lazarus. How frustrated his sisters must have been waiting on Jesus . . . waiting for a miracle. And how disheartened and defeated they must have felt when He didn't come and Lazarus died. Jesus had already informed His uncomprehending disciples, however, that "this sickness is not unto death,"*(John 11:4 KJV)* but that He was allowing it to happen to reveal His glory. Four days too late by human standards, Jesus was still right on time. When He called Lazarus' name, life returned to the lifeless body and the man was completely restored. Not even death's limits are a match to God's power.

I won't say this is an easy lesson to learn. God has had to teach and reteach me on several occasions. I used to wonder as I read through the history of the Jewish nation in the Old Testament, "How could they forget all God had brought them through and doubt Him every time they faced a new problem?" He parted the ocean so they could walk through on dry ground, yet they complained, thinking they would starve to death. He rained bread from Heaven every morning for them to eat, yet they complained they would die of thirst. He drowned their enemies, gave them water from a rock, caused their clothes to never wear out, yet when they came to the land of Canaan, the land flowing with milk and honey, the place of abundance, the Promised Land . . . they complained because the people were too big. Why could they not see that the One who had been leading them was the God of the whole universe and that, with Him, nothing was impossible? No situation was too desperate. No ocean was too big. No nation was too powerful. It seems completely absurd to me. Then, I look at my own life, and I realize . . . He's brought me through so many things, opened so many doors, overcome so many obstacles and still, when I face the next seemingly unsurpassable hurdle, I sit down and whine in despair, thinking I've reached a dead end and that I can go no further.

I can think of two very memorable moments in which God reminded me that He is not constrained by such limits. The first occurred at the end of my freshman year as an undergraduate. I had left Lee University, the college I attended during my first semester, to attend a college closer to home. Both were Christian colleges with outstanding academic reputations, but there was one colossal difference . . . *God* had sent *me* to *Lee*. I transferred for several "justifiable" reasons, but the stark reality was that I was out of God's will . . . and I knew it. I had an opportunity to serve as praise and worship leader at my home church, something I'd dreamt of doing since I first began to play the keyboard several years earlier, but the timing was not God's timing. He was leading me into a learning phase, not a leading one. I didn't realize how important that step was in God's plan for me. I wanted to seize the opportunity while it was there, so I foolishly left the place to which I had been divinely appointed, the place where God had planted me in order to grow me into the spiritually mature person I needed to be in order to fulfill His purposes for my life, and went to the place where I could enter immediate service. It didn't take very long at all for me to realize the error of my ways, but it couldn't be undone. I was there, in a new college with no path by which to return to my former one, since by leaving, I'd forfeited my full tuition scholarship and could not afford to attend without it.

As I sought God, I repented, pleading with Him to help me find some way back, promising to never again leave a place where I knew He wanted me to be (a promise which I'm ashamed to say I've broken on more than one occasion). I researched scholarship information only to conclude that the scholarship I had been awarded could, under no circumstances, be reinstated upon departure from the university. I was discouraged. I had ignorantly chosen a path of my own discretion that had taken me out of God's will and landed me in a place of discontentment, in which I was now stuck . . . with no way out. I continued to deepen my relationship with the Lord under these not so favorable circumstances, and He used me in spite of my disobedience. He grew me in several ways,

---

but I still felt out of place; knowing I was meant to be somewhere totally different, both physically and spiritually.

When the time came to register for the coming semester of college, God said, "No." I heard that edict clearly, although I didn't completely understand it. I desperately *wanted* to go back to Lee, but I didn't really see any way. I emailed my advisor there, inquiring whether there were any other scholarships that I could apply for as a transfer student, but I knew from my own research that the financial possibilities of my returning to Lee were . . . well . . . impossible. I couldn't go back to Lee, but God was instructing me not to register for classes where I was; so what was I supposed to do? Wait on God. One of the best, yet possibly most difficult, concepts imaginable. Wait on God. I didn't have time to wait. The registration deadline was approaching . . . here . . . gone. Roadblock. Dead end. But God . . . what a powerful phrase . . . BUT GOD opened a door!

Now that the deadlines were passed and my own efforts were exhausted, I received my advisor's reply.

"I have great news! Never before has this happened, but the president of the university has agreed to reinstate your [full tuition] scholarship."

So tell me, is anything too hard for the Lord? *(Genesis 18:14; Jeremiah 32:27)*

I didn't understand why God kept saying "wait", but I'm so glad He did; because HE showed me that the limitations that bind all my efforts are nothing in comparison to His divine authority. Even when I am disobedient, He is faithful and able to set me back on track. Where He leads me, He will clear the way.

Another notable revelation of God's limitless ability took place several years later. To most, it would seem a rather unremarkable occurrence . . . not even the kind of thing they'd expect God to be concerned with. But God is concerned with those things that concern us . . . the little things in our lives that matter to us.

My husband, Shane, had landed a new job with an offshore drilling company. He had not yet been assigned to a rig, however; and was told that, since he could be assigned internationally, he would have a better chance at an immediate start date if he had a passport. That shouldn't have been a problem since we'd been doing international summer mission trips since our marriage nearly six years earlier . . . but . . . we'd misplaced his passport. We really needed him to begin work as soon as possible, because our finances were quickly dwindling; so we scheduled an appointment with a passport agency in New Orleans, Louisiana—a four hour drive from our home.

Shane is not much on paperwork or navigation, so I took off from my job for a day and found a baby sitter so that we could leave early and make the trip. We had everything under control—documents in hand, appointment made, GPS set—until . . . we got lost. Yes, my navigation skills (along with my ability to read the GPS, apparently) failed and sent us nearly an hour off course. I got online on my I Pad to change the appointment time from 11:30 to 12:30, but to my horror, I discovered that the agency's daily hours of operation were 8:00-12:00.

We had driven four hours . . . almost five now, *and* I'd lost a day of work, and we were *not* going to get a passport. I tried in vain to contact someone in the agency office, but the number listed was a national hotline which awarded me the privilege of talking to an automated message center. It was hopeless. We had wasted our time, money, efforts and hope. Really, the most sensible thing to do now was to turn around and head home, instead of continuing our fruitless advance into unknown, crowded territory.

But I felt the still, calm voice of God saying, "Trust Me. Do you trust Me?" In my heart I felt my answer, "Yes, but . . ." No. No buts. We cannot trust God with a but. The "buts" do not apply to Him. There are no limits, deadlines, restrictions or even CLOSED times that apply to Him. We had to keep going. My mind, still blinded by the roadblocks in front of me, began to scramble the pages of reason to figure out how God might be planning to work this out. Maybe the time on the Internet was wrong—yeah right—this is a government web page. Maybe we will somehow make this last thirty minute stretch in fifteen minutes and get there right on time. God could do that. That one was promising right up until the clock read 12:10. So there just was no way. Still, as the gas light flashed "low fuel" and Shane gave the signal to turn into a gas station, I prodded him on. "No, we have to get there." Despite the "no-way" situation we were in, I felt God's urgent beckon to trust Him and continue. So continue we did. We found the building at 12:15, but it took another ten minutes to locate the correct tower, floor and room. When we finally stepped off the elevator at 12:25, the confirmation of our dreaded outcome stared us in the face. On the glass doors that served as the corridor to the U.S. Passport Agency, in bold letters, our defeat glared at us.

UNITED STATES PASSPORT AGENCY
HOURS OF OPERATION: 8-12

We stopped in our tracks, defeated. Shane said, "Let's go." But I said, "We have to at least try the door." We did . . . and . . . it opened! The officer inside asked if we had an appointment. I began apologizing for our tardiness, but he just smiled, said "Don't worry about it," and waved us on in. Again, God had broken through the impossible roadblocks that stood between us and our need.

How many times have you stood at a door, deemed it locked and impossible to enter, turned around and left? How close were you to a breakthrough . . . to complete success? Don't listen to the limits proclaimed by your surroundings. Listen to God. Trust Him. "Greater is He that is in you than he that is in the world." *(I John 4:4 KJV)* God opens doors that seem forever shut. He makes a way where there is no way. You may be standing on the threshold of a miracle. Just *try the door.*

CHAPTER 10

He'll stay awake for you

few nights ago, a very severe storm passed through our area. My husband was at work, so I was home alone with our four children. I woke to the sound of thunder and to vast amounts of lightning. A quick survey of my surroundings told me that the lightning was close and that we were experiencing tornado-type weather. Since my baby boy's bed is against a window, I moved him into the bed with me. Then, after a few more minutes, I decided I needed to move my girls downstairs into my room as well in case we needed to take cover quickly. I admit that I was a little concerned as to how I'd get them all to safety quickly; but I laid them down on the floor by my bed with pillows and blankets, said a prayer and went back to bed. My four year old daughter asked me about the storm, and I told her that I needed to keep them away from the windows because the lightening was pretty bad, but I assured her that everything was all right. Then she asked me a question that absolutely astounded me. She said, "Mommy, will you stay awake for us?" I expected her to say, "I'm scared," or "Can we sleep in your bed," but her only concern was whether I'd be awake. I told her that I'd stay awake for them, and I didn't hear another word out of any of them. They slept peacefully, seemingly oblivious to the storm around us.

Wow! If only we could trust God the way she trusted me. She felt safe as long as I was awake to watch out for them.

In the gospel of Mark, we find Jesus and His disciples in the midst of a furious storm. Beaten by the waves, the disciples became fearful. They were even more upset to discover their Master asleep in the stern. They aroused Him from His sleep and questioned, "Teacher, don't you care if we drown?" *(Mark 4:38b NIV)* Jesus, probably perturbed at being awakened from His peaceful sleep, got up and hushed the storm. Then He asked His friends, "Why are you so afraid? Do you still have no faith?" *(Verse 40)*

In the midst of the storm, the disciples failed to realize that the Master of the wind and waves was in their boat. He could sleep soundly, because He knew that His Father held His life in His hands, and that this storm was no match for His supreme authority and power.

The Bible tells us in Psalm 121:3-4 that "He who keeps [us] will not slumber or sleep." No matter how strong the storm is that is going on around us, God is awake and watching over us. He will protect us and will not let us be destroyed. Rest in Him and let Him be your refuge. Our worrying cannot protect us from the storm. As a matter of fact, our worrying cannot accomplish anything at all. *(Which of you by worrying can add one cubit to his stature? Matthew 6:27 NKJV)* Instead, "Cast all your anxiety on Him because He cares for you." *(I Peter 5:7 NIV)*

Psalm 46:10 instructs us to, "Be still, and know that I am God." *(NIV)* The Hebrew meaning of this verse is literally to "let go" or "release" and know that God is in control. Take your hands off your stormy situation, and allow God to guide you to safety. He will stay awake for you.

CHAPTER 11

The greatest peace comes when you release your greatest fears to God

*For God hath not given us the spirit of
fear; but of power, and of love, and of a sound
mind. II Timothy 1:7 KJV*

*He stilled the storm to a whisper; the
waves of the sea were hushed. Psalm 107:29
NIV*

As a child, I was terribly afraid of bad weather. My worst fear was that a tornado would rip through, destroying everything and taking our lives. I am not sure why I developed such a fear. We live in an area that often faces tornado type weather, but I had never actually been in a tornado.

In elementary school, I would always call home sick when the tornado bell sounded. My mom would drive 30 minutes through the terrible weather conditions to pick me up from school and take me home. Although her driving through the weather probably wasn't the wisest idea, I understand now that she knew the real source of my problem; and she wanted me to feel safe.

The fear didn't end in my elementary years. I took it with me to junior high school. Each time the tornado bell sounded, that same sick feeling rose in the pit of my stomach. One day, however, everything changed. I remember the day vividly. The tornado bell sounded around 10:00 that morning, and we all filed into the hallways of Carthage Junior High. I asked for permission to call home, because I was terribly sick at my stomach. I called, and my mom arrived promptly to pick me up and take me with her to my dad's business. When I arrived at the warehouse (that's what we called the place), everyone was doing business as usual, not paying much attention to the weather. I didn't understand why they weren't making a big deal out of this situation. The tornado sirens were sounding! Hello! I couldn't shake the feeling of panic and fear. I decided to seek comfort from my little Precious Moments New Testament Bible. I went outside, and, looking up at the ominous clouds above, I opened my Bible to a random passage. It opened to Psalm 107, and I began to read. When I reached verse 29, my life changed. I slowly read the words, *"He maketh the storm a calm, so that the waves thereof are still." (KJV)*

Immediately, the storm inside me was stilled. A peace came over me like I'd never experienced; and looking up again, I noticed a beauty like no other in those storm clouds. I told my mom I was ready to go back to school. She took me back, but the principal said I didn't need to go to my 4th period class since the bell would ring soon. He sent me to sit in the counselor's office and wait for the bell. The counselor wasn't there, so I reached on her shelf and took her Bible, eager to read the words once more.

I never called home again when the tornado bell rang. I never sensed the slightest fear in the ominous weather. In fact, a few weeks later, tornado watches covered our county on a Sunday night around the time for church to start. Worried members were coming in, keeping their eyes on the weather outside. I stood at the front porch of the church, peacefully admiring the works of God as I sang quietly to myself the beautiful worship song, *"I stand, I stand in awe of You ... I stand, I stand in awe of You ... Holy God to whom all praise is due ... I stand in awe of You."* I truly meant it. Where I'd once stood in fear, I could now stand in awe; because one day, I turned to God in the face of my fear, and He made my storm a calm. He stilled the storm to a whisper in which I found His sweet and awesome presence. Since that time, when the weather gets stormy, I sense the awesomeness of God and I can't help but thank Him for His greatness and for delivering me from my deepest fears.

Fear comes at unexpected times and through many different avenues. The enemy seeks to use fear to destroy us and prevent us from fulfilling God's calling on our lives. Fear blinds us and binds the faith necessary to live in God's perfect will.

I will never forget the night that fear began its threat to detour me from the path God was leading me into. I was sitting in the nosebleed section in the Tennessee Volunteers basketball arena in mid-March for a youth conference known as Winterfest. The speaker was Jensen Franklin, and the title of his message was 9-11. I don't remember much else about the message. He used the tragic events of September 11, 2001 to illustrate his message. When he showed one of the crashes on the screen, fear gripped me with a sudden sharp stab. I was scheduled to leave in June going on my very first mission trip to Nicaragua. I was excited, because I'd always wanted to participate in a short term mission trip. However, I felt a shadow of death creep over me as I watched the crash in the video. The enemy began to plant in my mind fear . . . . Fear that my plane would crash . . . Fear that I'd never come back . . . Fear that this mission trip would be my final and fatal work of ministry.

Throughout the months that followed, I tried to suppress the fear and focus on the excitement of my approaching adventure. I was able to keep the thoughts of fear to a minimum beneath all the other emotions and preparations of the trip. The morning of my departure, however, it all resurfaced in a flood of fear and doubt and a sense of certain doom. I called my best friend, crying, pleading for prayer and help out of what seemed certain death. I actually let the fear take such hold of me that I felt as if God was warning me that this would be a trip of martyrdom. Still, I knew of a certainty that it was God's will for me to participate in this trip, and nothing was going to stop me.

On the plane the next morning, the fears had not subsided. There were over 50 members in our team, but I was seated next to a total stranger. I had no idea that this "stranger" would be God's agent to change my life yet again through the face of my worst fears. We had to taxi for a while on the runway, so I opened my Bible to II Timothy 1:7 seeking comfort in the words *"For God hath not given us the spirit of fear; but of power, and of love, and of a sound mind." (KJV)* I began to feel some relief, but the heaviness remained. The stranger beside me saw me reading, pulled out his Bible and asked me to see if I could read it. I looked over to see a Spanish Bible. At the time, I knew absolutely no Spanish, but the sight of the Bible initiated a very worthwhile conversation. The man was from Honduras but had been serving in the U.S. military. He was going home to visit his family for a while. He asked me the reason of my trip and began to encourage me that I could never possibly know the impact my week in Nicaragua would have on the people of the villages we'd visit. I felt complete confirmation that God had sent me there and that, as my stranger friend assured me, He would change my life through the experience. I looked out the window of the plane as we began to speed down the runway. As we lifted from the ground, I again felt the overwhelming and unfathomable peace of God fill my whole being. I knew that everything would be all right. Since then, I have been to Nicaragua on ten such trips and to Honduras on one; and every time the plane leaves the runway, I sense that same peace . . . that awe . . . that brings tears to my eyes and joy to my soul. That trip, by the way, became the beginning of my realization that God was calling me (and now my entire family) to fulltime mission work in Nicaragua. What if I had let fear keep me on the ground?

CHAPTER 12

God wants NONE OF YOUR BUSYNESS!

Perhaps one of the greatest plagues of today's society is busyness. I'll be the first to admit that my usual answer to the age-old question, "How have you been?" is . . . "Busy."

While we definitely don't need to be lazy or idle, "too busy" can also be a real problem. We can become too busy to see the needs around us, too busy to take notice of our family, too busy to function clearly, even too busy to keep our sanity!

Even Jesus saw the importance of taking a break, of stepping back and breaking away to be alone with the Father. In Mark 6:31, He beckoned His disciples to "come with me by yourselves to a quiet place and get some rest." *(NIV)* The disciples had been busily ministering alongside Jesus. He was calling them away for a while to rest before continuing their ministry in Bethsaida. Later in this same chapter, (verse 46), Jesus left the disciples to go up on a mountain to pray. The night of His arrest, as Jesus prepared for His crucifixion, He took Peter, James and John with Him to the Garden of Gethsemane for a time of prayer. Each time He came "down from the mountain", He did mighty things. He knew that, before He could minister, He needed to receive strength from the Father. In order for us to have something to give in ministry, we have to get alone with God and allow Him to strengthen and fill us.

Even if all the tasks that keep us busy are noble things . . . maybe even ministries . . . we have to stop and rest occasionally and be refreshed, renewed and reminded of our purpose. In Jesus' case, all of His busyness was ministry, but He still needed a break for Himself and the disciples every now and then. We need to "break away" to be refreshed and renewed, to be refilled with God's power, and to keep a proper perspective.

Be refreshed/renewed.

Matthew 11:28-30 says, "Come to me, all you who are weary and burdened, and I will give you rest. Take my yoke upon you and learn from me, for I am gentle and humble in heart, and you will find rest for your souls. For my yoke is easy and my burden is light." *(NIV)* Jesus knew that we would become tired . . . physically and mentally exhausted . . . at times. That is why He encouraged us in these verses to come to Him, to lay down our burdens, and get in the yoke with Him . . . allow Him to help carry the weight.

From the beginning of time, rest has been part of God's design for mankind. He gave us this example when He created the earth. *("By the seventh day God had finished the work He had been doing; so on the seventh day He rested from all His work." Genesis 2:2 NIV)* Certainly God didn't need to rest, but He was laying an example for His creation. He even worked a time of rest into His creation . . . on day one! *("God called the light 'day,' and the darkness he called 'night.'" Genesis 1:5 KJV)* He provided night as a time for man to rest from his work. It is physically necessary for us to occasionally take time away from all our hectic tasks and be still . . . REST.

Be refilled.

Just as Jesus would get away to spend time with the Father before ministering to the multitudes, we must get alone and spend time with God, allowing Him to refill us daily. Remember that we can do nothing by our own strength; therefore, we need God to strengthen us and fill us. When Jesus ascended to

Heaven following His resurrection, He instructed His disciples, ". . . but stay in the city until you have been clothed with power from on high." *(Luke 24:49 NIV)* He had already commanded them to witness to all nations, but He now told them to do **nothing** until they had received the power of the Holy Ghost. If we intend to be effective witnesses, we must stop and wait for God to refill us with His power.

Be reminded. (Keep a proper perspective.)

Sometimes we become so overwhelmed with all that we have to do, all the roles that we are trying to fill, that we forget *why* we are doing it all. We forget the purpose that drives our work, and the Lord who is the source of our strength. By stepping away from it all, we allow God to speak to us and remind us of His vision for our lives, the vision that drives us forward. Sometimes that vision can become blurred underneath our busy lives, but a little alone time in His presence puts it all back in focus. David prayed in Psalm 25:4-5, "Show me your ways, o Lord, teach me your paths; guide me in your truth and teach me . . ." *(NIV)* God will guide us and keep us on track, but we have to pay attention . . . and that means being still . . . being quiet . . . being in His presence, free from distractions.

> "As Jesus and his disciples were on their way, he came to a village where a woman named Martha opened her home to him. She had a sister called Mary, who sat at the Lord's feet listening to what he said. But Martha was **distracted by all the preparations** that had to be made. She came to him and asked, 'Lord, don't you care that my sister has left me to do the work by myself? Tell her to help me!'
>
> "'Martha, Martha,' the Lord answered, 'You are worried and upset about many things, but few things are needed—or indeed only one. Mary has chosen what is better, and it will not be taken away from her.'" *Luke 10:38-42 NIV*

Martha was doing a *good* thing. She was tending to the "needs" of her very special guest. But in so doing, she was missing out on intimate time that she, like Mary, could have been spending at the feet of Jesus. Jesus wasn't interested in the perfect evening that Martha was trying to ensure. He was interested, (just as He is now with us), in relationship. Martha was distracted by her chores and missed a great opportunity. There will always be things that need to be done, but they can wait. We will never *find* the time to sit at Jesus' feet. We have to just lay everything else aside and *make* the time.

Pay Attention

When we are too busy, we often miss the needs of those around us. Maybe we're too busy to notice someone's hurt or need; or maybe we just decide we don't have time to stop and help. How many times do we pray, "Lord, help them" when we could do something for them ourselves? Maybe we are the one that God has sent to help minister to their need; but we say a little prayer and keep going, leaving their needs unmet. It is crucial that we, as Christians, take time to notice and to minister to the spiritual and physical needs around us.

Jesus was never too busy to minister to others. According to Mark 6, as Jesus was withdrawing from the crowd, He turned around to see the multitudes following Him. The Bible says He was "moved with compassion." He stopped what He was doing and taught them and fed them before leaving that place.

In John 4, Jesus passed through Samaria on His way to Galilee because there was one woman there who needed an encounter with the Messiah. Because of their conversation at the well, many Samaritans believed on Him. *("Many of the Samaritans from that town believed in him because of the woman's testimony, 'He told me everything I ever did.' So when the Samaritans came to him, they urged him to stay with them, and he stayed two days. And because of his words many more became believers." John 4:39-41 NIV)*

In the gospel of Luke, Jesus accounts a story we commonly title "The Good Samaritan":

> *In reply Jesus said: "A man was going down from Jerusalem to Jericho, when he was attacked by robbers. They stripped him of his clothes, beat him and went away, leaving him half dead. A priest happened to be going down the same road, and when he saw the man, he passed by on the other side. So too, a Levite when he came to the place and saw him, passed by on the other side. But a Samaritan, as he traveled, came where the man was; and when he saw him, he took pity on him. He went to him and bandaged his wounds, pouring on oil and wine. Then he put the man on his own donkey, brought him to an inn, and took care of him. The next day he took out two denarii and gave them to the innkeeper. 'Look after him,' he said, 'and when I return, I will reimburse you for any extra expense you may have.'" Luke 10:25-35 NIV*

Each of the first two men turned his head, passed by and went on his way, ignoring the man's need. The third man, the "good neighbor", sacrificed of his money and time to meet the hurting man's need. We need not be in such a hurry that we don't have time to stop and help someone in need.

> *'For I was hungry and you gave me nothing to eat, I was thirsty and you gave me nothing to drink, I was a stranger and you did not invite me in, I needed clothes and you did not clothe me, I was sick and in prison and you did not look after me.' "They will also answer, 'Lord, when did we see you hungry or thirsty or a stranger or needing clothes or sick or in prison, and did not help you?'" "He will reply, 'Truly I tell you, whatever you did not do for one of the least of these, you did not do for me.'" Matthew 25:42-45 NIV*

It is incredibly hard to hear the voice of God over the roar of our hectic schedules. It's okay to take a break. In fact, it's necessary. Rest. Be still. Be quiet. Listen. Pay attention.

CHAPTER 13

God passionately desires relationship with you

Throughout the Word of God are found various promises for the people of God. We love to claim those promises, and rightfully so. Let me draw your attention to a passage from Leviticus 26:

> "Do not make idols or set up an image or a sacred stone for yourselves, and do not place a carved stone in your land to bow down before it. I am the Lord your God. Observe my Sabbaths and have reverence for my sanctuary. I am the Lord. If you follow my decrees and are careful to obey my commands, I will send you <u>rain in its season</u>, and the

ground will yield its crops and the trees their fruit. Your threshing will continue until grape harvest and the grape harvest will continue until planting, and you will eat all the food you want and live in safety in your land. I will grant peace in the land, and you will lie down and no one will make you afraid. I will remove wild beasts from the land, and the sword will not pass through your country. You will pursue your enemies, and they will fall by the sword before you. Five of you will chase a hundred, and a hundred of you will chase ten thousand, and your enemies will fall by the sword before you. I will look on you with favor and make you fruitful and increase your numbers, and I will keep my covenant with you. You will still be eating last year's harvest when you will have to move it out to make room for the new. I will put my dwelling place among you, and I will not abhor you. I will walk among you and be your God, and you will be my people. I am the Lord your God, who brought you out of Egypt so that you would no longer be slaves to the Egyptians; I broke the bars of your yoke and enabled you to walk with heads held high." (Verses 1-13 NIV)

In this passage alone, God promises prosperity, protection, peace, victory over enemies, productivity, abundance and relationship. As you read this passage, which of these promises appeals to you most? What is it that you really desire from God? What is most often the subject of your prayers?

As God challenged me with this question, I began to think about my prayer life, my desires, and my preoccupations. I felt that God was asking me, "Do you desire one or all of these promises more than you desire ME?" I discovered that, when I begin to seek the blessings of God more than relationship with God, I find myself frustrated and out of focus.

Specifically, when I am seeking prosperity or financial security, I am constantly stressed about money and things. I cannot seem to make the budget work no matter how hard I try . . . and just when I think I have it all under control, some unexpected expense pops up.

When my primary concern is protection, I find myself praying somewhat obsessively for the safety and well-being of my family. I become paranoid every time they leave the house, worried that something might happen before they return. While I believe that God intends for us to pray for protection over our family, I do not believe that He wills us to be fearful. After all, II Timothy 1:7 says, "For God hath not given us the spirit of fear; but of power, and of love, and of a sound mind." *(KJV)*

When I'm constantly praying for victory, I'm binding myself in my own mind, tangled in the defeat that comes by trusting in my own control rather than surrendering completely to God.

When I'm seeking God, however, and my utmost desire is to know Him more, to experience His presence more deeply and to hear His voice more clearly, these other concerns seem to disappear . . . not because I no longer care about these things, but because I become totally engrossed in Him . . . and He takes care of all those other things, just like He said He would!

We are human beings, and we have needs. God expects us to pray about them and to ask for them. He said, "You do not have because you do not ask God." *(James 4:2 NIV)* Once we have made our needs known, however, we should trust Him to provide for them. *("But my God shall supply all your need according to his riches in glory by Christ Jesus." Philippians 4:19 KJV)* If we seek Him first, we will truly find that He'll provide all that we need . . . even the needs we have not yet realized that we possess! *("But seek first His kingdom and His righteousness and all these things will be given to you as well." Matthew 6:33 NIV)*

So what is it that you want from God? Prosperity, protection, victory, peace . . . or relationship? He desires relationship with you . . . passionately . . . so much so that He sent His only begotten Son that whoever believes in Him will not perish but have everlasting life . . . in Heaven . . . with Him. *(John 3:16 paraphrased)*

NOW WHAT?

I hope that as you've read through these lessons of my life, you have found something helpful to apply to your own life . . . maybe even to your current situation. Even more so, I hope that you have been encouraged to seek God and to listen to Him as He speaks into your own life. Maybe you have even been reminded of some lessons He has taught you that you can share with someone else.

Or maybe you've discovered that you don't yet have a relationship with the Father of my lessons. You know who God is, but you don't really *know* Him. If this is true, you can know Him today . . . right now. The Bible says that if we confess with our mouths that Jesus Christ is Lord and believe in our hearts that God has raised Him from the dead (for our forgiveness), then we will be saved. *(Romans 10:9 paraphrased)* This simply means that if you will surrender your life to the lordship of Jesus Christ—inviting Him to live in your heart, and believing that He came, lived and died to forgive your sins—He will become your Savior, and you will inherit the greatest promise He has to offer . . . relationship with God and eternal life with Him in Heaven. And the best news is . . . your journey has just begun!

Like any relationship, you will experience easy times and hard times in your relationship with the Lord; times when you can feel the arms of God wrapped around you, and times when you wonder where He is; times when you can hear His voice and feel His hand clearly guiding you, and times when you really have to press in and seek Him. It's all part of the journey of getting to know God and His perfect plan for your life, and every stage in this journey is absolutely beautiful . . . completely amazing.

ABOUT THE AUTHOR

Kerri Estes was raised in a Christian home in a small town in Mississippi. She has been involved in various ministries in her church, including the youth ministry, praise and worship team, and evangelism ministries. She and her husband, Shane, are currently pursuing God's calling on their lives to enter the foreign mission field. Their desire is to work with the young people of Nicaragua.

Kerri's passion has always been working with young people. This passion, along with her passion to reach Spanish-speaking peoples with the message of Jesus Christ, has led to her current occupation of high school Spanish teacher. In addition to her involvement in her church and her career, Kerri is the mother to four children: Jeylan, Deznee, Pheebie, and Jaxsen.

Kerri has been collecting stories of God's faithfulness throughout her pursuit of His will for her life. With this book, she is finally ready to share them. Her desire for this book is that it will encourage others to pursue God's calling on their lives without fear and that it will especially impact her own children as they see through its pages God's continued faithfulness.

Printed in the United States
By Bookmasters